Jake Plants Grapes

by Tristan Horrom
illustrated by Eva Vagreti

Decodable 14

McGraw Hill Education

Bothell, WA • Chicago, IL • Columbus, OH • New York, NY

MHEonline.com

Send all inquiries to:
McGraw-Hill Education
8787 Orion Place
Columbus, OH 43240

ISBN: 978-0-02-145562-1
MHID: 0-02-145562-7

Printed in China

10 11 12 13 14 DSS 28 27 26 25 24

"You can plant grapes," said Mom.

"Jake, take that and dig."

"Plant that grape bud, Jake."

Jake did not see grapes.

"Jake, can you see big red grapes?" said Mom.

Mom and Jake ate big red grapes!